Is He Really A 10?

By

Jan-Marie Wells

Is He Really A 10?

R&E Publishers
P.O. Box 2008
Saratoga, CA 95070
TEL: (408) 866-6303
FAX: (408) 866-0825

LC 91-52956

I.S.B.N. 0-88247-885-0

Cover Art by Janet Simmonds
Typesetting by Diane Parker

Dedication

To My Sons Terry and Brent,

Believe in yourself and remember integrity
will make you a prince among men.

From Mom with all my love.

CONTENTS

1 INTRODUCTION

Do you ever wonder why your serious relationships with women end? Have you ever sat down and really been honest with yourself and asked yourself, "Would I date me?" If you have a hard time being insightful, then maybe you need to take inventory and just see if there are any socially unacceptable habits you may want to consider improving. Have you forgotten all those (seemingly unimportant) "lessons in manners" that your mother taught you? If so, then you could probably use a good "brush-up" which is exactly what this book can give you.

This book has been written to appeal to men and their logic. It is direct, honest and its contents target the many subjects that people think about but never want to talk about. It is neither a male-bashing book nor a sexist book. It was not written to be malicious, but out of love and concern for those men who do not understand why they keep making the same mistakes with women. Men do not like to change but they sure do like a challenge...

So, why not take the challenge and see if there are any significant things about yourself which you could improve? Believe it or not, it is the little things that your mother tried to teach you that are important to women. Has the woman in your life been nagging you about little things that annoy her? You may want to try and improve these little things—it will not only make her happier, but (and you may be surprised) will also make you feel better and more confident about yourself.

2 CHEMISTRY AND INITIAL CONTACT

He has dreamed about her, fantasized about meeting her and then, one day, "poof," she appears. "That is it," he says to himself. "That is what I want, right there." This is physical attraction, not chemistry. The chemistry is what happens when you learn to like someone and that takes time. It is whether or not you really can, and do, blend well. This is what happens when the relationship works.

And now he is wondering if she is going to like him, right? I would say her first impression of him in their initial contact will generally determine his chances of whether or not he will see her again. So, he must try and be relaxed and ask her about herself. Do not ask her what kind of car she drives or if she owns her home or how well her job pays. This type of questioning will put up her "this guy is bad news" antennae. Ask her if she likes to travel, shop, or ski. Ask her about the last book she read, if she likes to go to the beach, what was the last movie she saw and about her family, etc. He doesn't want to be an obnoxious, insecure braggart and tell her all about his personal possessions (his car, house, boat, airplane, etc.). This will tell her that he is insecure about himself. Women don't want to be with really insecure men. Be humble and even a little secretive. He needs to let things come out slowly about his personal life. Talk more in generalities. Women love humility and mystery in a man. He wants her to like him for who he is, not for what he owns. And if she is too interested in these personal things—well, guess what? She is a sniffing gold-digger. Better beware—this is not a good sign. Better to punt than continue with his pass. So, he needs to pick himself up, dust himself off, and start all over again....

3 THE DATING AND WAITING GAME

He has decided that the attraction is good, and he is interested enough to ask her for a date. When he asks her on a first date, he should tell her to meet him at a designated place so that both of them have their own means of transportation. An "ideal" first date is for lunch in a well-lit room. This way, it is non-threatening for either one of them. If it ends up that neither of them like each other, then they are not stuck with each other for the ride home. If lunch is not possible, then how about having a cup of coffee or tonic water after work, for an hour? He should be specific—an hour. If he did not specify dinner and he spends more than an hour with her, then he should ask the lady if he may buy her dinner. She's probably starved.

The evening comes to a close. It's either been wonderful or ghastly. He walks her to her car and tells her good night. Now, here is the part where he has got to be fair. If he likes her and feels good enough about her to kiss her, he gives her a peck on the cheek, says good night, and maybe that he'd like to see her again soon. He might call her the next day and tell her that he had a good time and that he'd like to take her out on a "real date." If he didn't like her, then he should not give her false hopes and say, "I'll give you a call sometime." No, no, no. This is not fair. He should simply say good night and that is it. There is nothing more hurtful than for a man to say that he will call, and then doesn't. He wouldn't want her to do this to him, would he? I'm sure he has called a lady that he was interested in, and maybe she didn't return his call. He didn't feel too good about it, I'm sure. It is the very same thing here. So, let's play the game fairly. If he is not interested, then he should not lead her on. That is cruel and unnecessary. She will respect him more if he does not lead her on. It won't give her the "ammunition" to tell her friends that he was a real jerk. He certainly does not want to get the bad rap of "well, he said he'd call me and he didn't—another jerk!"

4 THE PARTY GIRL VS. THE NESTER

The "style" of woman for him will depend on where he is in his life. He may be at a place where he doesn't want anything too serious, so he may seek out the "Party Girl." This is the woman who stays out late a lot, drinks too much and just wants to "raise hell" all the time. She is not the type that he wants to settle down with and have a family.

The "Party Girl" frequents bars on a regular basis. She knows the bartenders and they know what to pour her to drink. Now, I am not saying that he can't meet a "good woman" at a bar. They are out there but he needs to be careful. If he watches and observes the lady, he will be able to see if she has a "Jekyll and Hyde" personality when she is drinking. This is an indication of trouble. It could mean she has an addiction to drinking, or some other deeper problems which he doesn't need.

If he is looking for a committed, one-on-one relationship, then he will be looking for "The Nester." This is the lady who just wants to "be" with him. She doesn't need to go out to dinner every night to an expensive restaurant or be "wined and dined," as some might say. She doesn't get out of control if she has a drink—she knows her limit and maintains it. She doesn't use drugs, either. She is a "happy camper," likes herself, can laugh at herself and is a true complement to her man. She is a lady in public and fun and deliciously delightful when she is alone with him. She's out there looking for you! Believe me....

5 MR. TOO AGGRESSIVE

He won't take "no" for an answer. On their first date, they went out to dinner and he sat down right beside her. During dinner, he put his hand on her thigh. This made her very nervous. He wouldn't keep his hands to himself, and she felt like he was mauling her. She would like to enjoy conversation with him, but she's so concerned and uncomfortable with his advances, she can't think of anything else.

These advances, which are too intimate, make her feel like all he is after, is sex. I'm sure he must know by now that women generally want to be thought of as a whole person—one who he is interested in getting to know, a woman with some brains, and not just for her body. She told him 'no', and he wouldn't take 'no' for an answer. The whole evening for her is ended before it even began because he didn't act like a gentleman and treat her like a lady. Instead, his advances were those of how he would treat a whore. If they were intimately involved and this happened, then that's a different thing. But hurried advances will always make a woman skeptical of his intentions, and whether or not they are honorable. It's not quite time to play "handsies" just yet! If she likes him, it will happen, some day.

6 HYGIENE

Everyone likes to be with a clean person. This means he bathes his body with soap daily, washes his hair with shampoo (not bar soap) daily. For the man who chooses to wash with only a bar of soap, I have news for him—a simple washcloth or brush removes more dirt than just soap alone. To wash his ears well he should use a cloth—otherwise blackheads will form inside his ears. And what woman wants to kiss a dirty ear? Ick! Cotton swabs work wonderfully in the folds of the ears (in order to get the soap out), and a little rubbing alcohol once or twice a week on a swab, just inside the ear (but not pushed into the ear canal) will remove the excess oil. If his skin tends to produce much excess oil, he might also want to try applying rubbing alcohol on cotton balls at least every other day, to remove the excess soap and oils on his back. He will be amazed at how much dirt there is, even after showering.

Does he know it's the 1990's and men need to use some type of deodorant? If he is one of those who does not care for deodorant (due to allergic reactions, etc.), he should try the "natural method" and use the mineral salt rocks from the department stores. They are great and really work well.

He makes excuses that the one place he hardly ever finds the time to visit is the dentist...The dentist needs to be one of the most important people in his life. He only has one set of adult teeth, and it is a crying shame not to have all of them lined up in a row without empty spaces in between them (the cause of many other dental problems).

Dentists have said that many men have bad breath due to old fillings, plaque build-up, or sometimes, he may have stomach problems. He should fit a visit to the dentist into his schedule once every six months, and not any less frequently than once a year. Great smiles do not have to be straight. Clean teeth and breath will do just fine!

Now that he has become older, he may notice that new hair is now appearing in places it never grew before—in his ears, nose, and coarser, longer hairs on his eyebrows. Keep these little darlings tweezed or cut off. Just because he started growing hair in these places does not mean that he needs to keep them there. Also, the hair on his neck should be shaved off between haircuts. It looks scruffy to see a man with a lot of hair on his neck. He will be able to go longer between haircuts if he removes it at least once a week. For his neck and sideburns, he can use some soap or shaving cream, a hand-held mirror and a razor, or purchase a cordless trimmer at a beauty supply store for about $35.

As far as cologne and aftershave are concerned...too much is tacky, tacky, tacky! He simply needs to put a little bit of his cologne behind his ears, on the back of his neck, in the center of his wonderful chest, and on his wrists.

Groomed men exude success...Grooming says "I like me, and I care enough about me to take the time to care for myself." It is a real turn-on to women. Believe it—it's true. Just ask one. A woman, that is.

7 THE EAR WAX CLEANER

He has forgotten that a cotton swab was to be used in the morning after he showered, to clean the ear wax out of his ears, because here he sits at his desk with his little finger crammed in his ear removing it. And, what does he do with the wax after he gets it out of there? Who knows? Doesn't he think he would be embarrassed if he got caught by someone who would care? I think he would.

8 THE NAIL-GNASHER AND TOENAIL-THRASHER

Chew and rip! That's the nail-gnasher and toenail-thrasher. The nail-gnasher always has his fingers in his mouth. He is constantly chewing his fingernails or his poor dried-out cuticles. Such a nasty habit. I suppose it sort of replaces that good ol' pacifier that Mom took away at age two.

Now envision this for a moment...A professional man, sitting at his large desk in his own office, across from a potential client, and he has his fingers in his mouth, chewing his fingernails. This does not give an impression of a calm, together guy, does it? Or, what is even more disgusting, is when he is pulling and chewing the cuticle around his fingernails. Hands are very visible and if he thinks he can hide his gnashed nails, guess what? He can't. He may decide he will only chew his fingernails in private. But unless he wears gloves, sits on his hands all the time, or puts them in his pockets, they do not disappear. When he reaches out to shake hands, or better yet, signs a contract, there they are, in all their glory, his "gnashed nails."

Germs live in damp, wet places and when he is constantly touching strange places that he does not know who else touched them, he leaves himself open to contracting infections when he puts his fingers in his mouth. Germs and viruses are transferred into his mouth via his hands. He should try and keep them out of his mouth, for his own good health.

And whatever gave him the idea that ripping off his toenails while watching T.V. was acceptable. This does not make for good romance, ever. His attempt at grooming should be done in the privacy of his bathroom with nail clippers over the trash can. Or, just maybe if he's lucky enough, she may pamper him with a pedicure. What a lucky guy!

9 THOSE SMELLY FEET

She's thinking his nose doesn't work, because every time he takes off those shoes of his, the room immediately takes on the odor of a boy's locker room.

First of all, it's not polite to take his shoes off in her presence unless she is a real steady date. And number two, if his feet do have odor, he needs to go to the market or drug store to purchase some deodorant foot spray or powder and put some in his shoes before he puts them on. It will also help to put it in his shoes while they're in the closet. Smelly shoes will make the rest of the clothes in the closet take on an awful odor, too.

There's nothing wrong with having good-smelling feet, especially if she has a foot fetish and loves to play with those little tootsies of his. Just because those feet are cooped up in those wingtips, loafers or tennies all day, doesn't mean they need to smell bad. Let's hear it for no more foot odor. Yeah!

10 THOSE INEXCUSABLE TABLE MANNERS

I'm sure you've had dinner with a group of people, and among them was the man that I'm going to tell you about right now. For lack of a better name, we'll call him "The Barbarian." He was the topic of conversation on the ride home after dinner and provided a few laughs for those who dined with him.

11 CLOTHING—YOUR BIGGEST STATEMENT

Did you ever hear the expression "Clothes Make the Man?" Well, believe it. Pressed and clean and odor-free is the right way to go. He can still be the "Mr. Rough and Tumble Guy" in his jeans and polo shirt, but they still should be clean. He may try and wear those shirts and sweaters more than once because he doesn't like to do laundry, or put out the money to have them laundered for himself. But if he is going to try to wear them more than once, he needs to check the armpits of the shirt for odor and see if they are odor-free. Nothing is worse than embracing a man whose shirt smells like body odor. This will definitely ruin the moment!

Does he ever check himself out in a full length mirror? What about from behind? Are his pants so stretched out in the rear-end that he looks like the little boy who just did a load in his drawers? This will happen if he has not had them cleaned and pressed in a while, if they are old and stretched out, or if he has lost weight. Whatever the reason, he should have them altered, get them cleaned, or throw them away.

He needs to be more aware of the fit of his clothes. He does not want them so tight that others can see the outline of the "bulge" in his pants. That's just as bad as the man with the baggy rear-end. And now, about his underwear? He does wear them, I hope, because it is more sanitary to do so. If he is not wearing them, then his whole unit is hanging down on one side, bouncing around. Why torture it? It does keep his jeans and slacks fresher if he does wear underwear. Don't you agree?

His clothes needn't be expensive to make a statement. In fact, when in doubt, he should wear a white oxford shirt and a pair of dark slacks and sport coat or leather jacket. This combination will make an acceptable statement in most circumstances anywhere, anytime.

Is he still trying to stay young by keeping remnants of his past in his closet? For example, his "Disco Danny" polyester bell-bottoms. Time to call the Goodwill. The rule here is, if he has not worn it in the past year, he needs to get rid of it. By the time it comes into fashion again, he will be too old to want to wear it anyway.

Now, when was the last time those shoes of his saw polish and a brush? How long has it been since they were taken to the shoe repair for new heels and soles? Many women *do* look at a man's shoes first—really. They figure if the shoes look bad, he is usually not too concerned about his appearance in general. This is a dead give-away for neatness or lack of it.

And how about those athletic shoes of his—are the shoe strings that were once white, now black? Well then, he should take them out and wash them with his whites. He does know that when he does his laundry, that he needs to separate his whites, darks, towels and sheets, correct? He does pre-spot with spot remover any stains on his clothes, because if he didn't, then after they are laundered, they are set in for good, so keep it handy and use it. His white socks and white underwear do go into one load in hot with bleach (that is, if he wants them to remain white), the light colors can go in another load in cold water, and the dark colors in another load, in cold water also. His bed sheets should not be washed with his towels either, unless he wants to get "fuzzies" all over his sheets. He should wash the furry rugs alone, too. He does not want to use hot dryers to dry his cotton. All cotton shirts look much better if they are put in the dryer for only about ten minutes and then hung out on plastic hangers to dry (wire hangers will rust on the shirts). This way, they will not shrink. Once the item is shrunk, that is it. He needs to give it to a smaller relative, because he will never fit in it again. And he needs to clean out those lint screens in the dryer, or he will be drying one load all day.

12 THE ADJUSTER

This man has his hands in his pockets, trying to do what? I really don't know if he does this nervously and does not realize that he is doing it, or if his shorts are too tight, or maybe not tight enough. Or is he just playing with his unit? I can't figure it out. Can you? He should really refrain from this display in public. It certainly makes women nervous around men who do this. Excusing himself from the situation or turning around would be a better way to handle this situation.

13 THE CHANGE JINGLER

Providing our own entertainment is something we all would like to have a say in, and not be at someone else's mercy. This man has no mercy. She is standing in line at the bank, and he is standing in line either in front of her or behind her. He has one or both of his hands in his pockets, jingling his change and keys. I guess he's trying to play a tune for her. But, she doesn't recognize the tune. She turns around and glares at him, but I don't think he gets the idea. It is bad enough that she has to stand in the bank line and wait, and wait, so let's do it quietly. Thanks...

14 MR. LOW PART

If Columbus was navigating on this man's head, he might have fallen off. This man's hair has thinned out and he feels that by parting his hair real low on the side and dragging the hair over, that she would not be able to tell he is losing his hair. Now what happens when he goes out in the wind and his hair blows up, or he goes swimming and all this stringy long hair is hanging in his face? More men have a problem with the idea of balding than women do. Some women find bald men very sexy and appealing. And, most women would rather have a man's hair shorter on the top and showing the thinness, rather than to see those silly low parts and hair that is dragged across his head and then plastered in place with gobs of hair spray. Thinner hair does not mean a man is less masculine. It just means his hair is getting thinner, and so what? Nobody cares, really—except him. He is still just as sexy.

15 TOO TIGHT

He does not seem to know the meaning of "tip" or gratuity. He embarrassed her for the last time. She can't even look the waitress in the eyes. Doesn't he know they make minimum wage and that people in the service business count on 10%-20% gratuity for their wages? Now, if the service was bad, that's a different story and questionable, but under any other circumstances, he should always leave a tip. This means tipping his barber or hair stylist, his manicurist, masseur, the waiter or waitress at the restaurant, the bellman at the hotel, the person who valets his car and to the person who details his car at the car wash. It's unfortunate, but the reality of tipping is, he'll be guaranteed a good job next time he frequents the establishment. And if he doesn't tip and they see him coming, they now know him as "Mr. Too Tight" and his service this time may be less than satisfactory. It may be a good idea for him to dig just a little bit deeper in his pockets to leave these people with a better impression.

Tipping = Better Service (next time).

16 THE OBNOXIOUS INSECURE BRAGGART

He's a label name-dropper and has to let her know how much he pays for what he wears and where he bought it. Does she really care? No, probably not, if she is a real squared-away person. And she doesn't care, and it bothers her that he does care so much.

He tells her all about the other great places where he has eaten when she's out to dinner with him; how these other restaurants were so much better than where they are dining right now. This will make her very uncomfortable, because he was with someone else. He can tell her about other restaurants in idle conversation, later. He has a date with her and should make it as pleasant an evening as possible, not talk about past dining experiences. He's told her all evening about his gorgeous ex-girlfriends or ex-wife, and all about his past, which she'd just as soon not hear about. His past is his past, and since she is his present lady of choice, she'd like to talk about them and their interests. Men need to refrain from talking too much about their pasts, good or bad!

17 THE GAS MAN

This is the worst, and he'll actually grin or laugh after he does it. And, he'll get this look on his face when she asks him "Did you let one?" "Who me?" he asks. He may think this is cool to do around the guys, but it's disgusting to do around his lady. The polite thing to do is to excuse himself from wherever he is (even if he is in bed) and head out of the room. This is not cute anymore, nor is it cool. Besides, the odor is enough to knock her out. If he does it too many times, she may do just that, knock him out (of her life, that is). Remember again, too much familiarity breeds contempt. He needs to excuse himself and leave the room.

18 THE MAN WHO DOESN'T RESPECT HER THINGS

She invited him over to her place and he showed up barefoot and wearing pants that were greasy and dirty. He had the nerve to walk in on her light-colored carpet and sit down on her white couch. Great guy, right? Barefeet get dirty with the oil that's excreted from the bottom of his feet mixed with the dirt from the pavement, which makes for one dirty carpet. It might be a good idea next time for him to wear his shoes over to her place, and then remove them inside her house. That would be the polite thing to do. And, as for the dirty pants, I don't think they are such a good idea either. He would be real offended if she ever got in his "new car" with grease on her shoes and got his carpet dirty, or sat with dirty pants on his light seats. Respecting each other's property is very important in the development of a relationship.

His feet don't belong propped up on her coffee table, or his keys thrown down on it for that matter. She spent her hard-earned money on her new furniture, and she doesn't want him to scratch it. It's new, and she'd like to enjoy it for awhile without any scratches. Glass table tops scratch and so does wooden furniture. The keys belong in his pockets, on the kitchen counter or on the floor. Scratching her table tops is like him getting his car keyed. This wouldn't make him happy one bit. Same deal. A scratch on her furniture is not any different than a scratch on his car. It makes everybody unhappy, those scratches. The only good scratches are back scratches.

19 THE GUM CHEWER

He appears to be more engrossed in his relationship with the gum in his mouth than with her conversation. He's chomping, cracking and snapping his gum, while she's trying to do business with him. When he chews gum, he may not want to be conducting business. It's very unprofessional, the chomping, popping and bubble-blowing and all! He needs to be alone with his gum, not conducting business with it. The affair he has with his gum need to be a rather private one. A nice ride in his car, or a day or evening alone would be great for him and his date...His gum.

20 ON THE ROAD AGAIN WITH THE NOSE PICKER

I guess this man never discovered Kleenex or handkerchiefs while he was growing up. Otherwise, why would this man, who is all dressed up, either going to or returning from the office, be driving with his index finger crammed up his nostril? He must think he is invisible. You must have seen this fellow, because there are a lot of them out there doing it. It must be boredom, or maybe it's a nervous habit. This man is driving down the I-5 interstate, "digging for gold" in his own car. Not real appealing to an onlooker. Now, come on, I mean really, guys. Is it really so difficult to either put a nice, white handkerchief in your pocket, or run to the local market and purchase a small box of tissue, and put it on the console or on the passenger side of the car? I think not.

Now, wouldn't he just die if Miss Wonderful pulled up next to him at the next traffic jam or intersection, and she looks over at him, and here he is with his finger crammed up his nose, digging for "gold," or whatever it is that he is after? He would probably feel like a real fool, and he should. Grown men know better...I think.

21 THE SNUFFLER

Sniff, snuffle, sniff, snuffle. This man has a drippy nose and instead of taking something to stop this drippy nose, he uses the back of his hand or the base of his wrist to wipe his nose. Another childlike behavior he carried over into adulthood.

If he doesn't care for the drowsy medications that are sold over-the-counter, he can call his physician and get a prescription that won't make him drowsy or leave him drippy anymore.

He's out to dinner, he forgot his allergy medicine and his allergies are acting up (he wouldn't knowingly have dinner with a bad cold and spread his germs.) He needs to blow his nose and he knows to do it quietly (no honking please!) and not to use his napkin. He remembered his nice white hankerchief, and he knows it's not just to use when he wants to surrender.

22 THE HAWKER AND SPITTER

Why does this happen? I think how he might have started doing this, was perhaps by watching the "men of the mound" hawk and spit between pitches. Quite a good possibility, don't you think? This is not a manly thing to do, and he does not really set a good example for the other little men who are watching him. And, he does not want to do it in the shower, either. What about trying to blow his nose in a Kleenex after he showers? No one wants to get in the shower after him and slip or stick to his nasal discharge. And he never wants to cover one side of his nose and blow it on the ground. He might want to carry a handkerchief or, a tissue works great and he can put tissue in his pockets. It's okay. He is not going to be less of a man because he chooses to use tissue...in fact, it is so much nicer when he does.

23 THE PERPETUAL DYSFUNCTIONAL WHINER

He blames everyone in his life—his parents, his boss, and you, for all of his mistakes and where he currently is, in his life. He has not yet learned how to take full responsibility for himself. And you say he's 40 years old. He needs to either see a psychologist and work through the problems he has not yet reconciled or seek out some group counseling. Any hospital would be a good place to begin to inquire for help. If he cannot afford treatment, they will help him find a support group that is right for him. A smart man asks for help...An ignorant man does not have enough common sense to ask!

24 THE THROAT CLEARER

Ugh-em, ugh-em, ugh-em; a nervous habit and the more he "ugh-em's" the more nervous he seems to be. He's probably not aware of it, and does it frequently. It is probably caused from post-nasal drip. A good antihistamine that won't make him drowsy would be a great idea. It would get rid of his problem very easily.

25 THE RELIGIOUS FANATIC

Hasn't everyone met this fellow? He reminds us of our favorite television evangelist, who is trying to save the world. He has a direct pipeline to God and he wants her to have it too, so every other sentence is a quote from the Bible. He has gone from being an addict of alcohol, drugs, women, etc., to being an addict of God. God does want this man to love him, worship him, live a good, clean life, and live the ten commandments. He does not want him to hide behind the Bible and use his teaching as a front or a vice. Setting an example makes people want to know what special "thing" he possesses that makes him a comforted, happy, well-adjusted, humble man. Being "pushy" about what God has done for him can be a real turnoff to others, especially if they just are not interested in knowing or learning about God from him. If he is a good example, others will follow, just like sheep. To make an appearance in God's house on Sunday is not good enough. What he hears and learns should be put into practice after he leaves. Church is not a social, making an appearance, or filling the pew. It is a religious experience, a holy one, and should be taken seriously. He should never use God as a device to gain.

26 THE TOE TAPPER

Tap, tap, tap. No, it's not a woodpecker at her side, it's the famous toe tapper. He does this to let others know that he is really not pleased about whatever situation he is involved in at that moment. It might be that he is standing in line waiting for something, and he's not being real patient. He tells her he hates standing in lines and she understands. But, guess what? This is the 90's, and waiting in lines is the name of the game. So, best he get used to it, otherwise he'll need to take those shoes into the shoe repair and have those holes in his soles fixed. It probably would save him some money if he learned how to be patient. Remember the old adage—"Patience is a virtue."

27 THE WRIST WATCH WATCHER

He's constantly looking at his wrist, checking the time. Not once or twice, but constantly. He's given her a low-browed dirty look, trying to let her know that because he's pressed for time and she may be running a little behind, that it's his time she's on, not hers. This pressure will only make her more nervous. He can let her know in a nice way that he is pressed for time. If he continues checking his watch it will only make sparks fly, and they won't be good sparks, because this will make her more intense and run further behind. So, stop watching that watch!

28 THE HORN HONKER

She's running around at the last minute, trying to take care of all the details before leaving the house, and he's all ready to go and sitting in the car honking the horn at her to hurry up. The appropriate thing for him to do in this situation, would be to ask her, "Honey, is there anything I can do to help you before we leave?" But he doesn't. He'd rather sit in the car and honk. Then he wonders why she's in a frenzy and so upset when they leave. He's made her angry by honking at her when she's in the house, trying to check the doors and windows to see if they are locked, shut off the coffee pot, unplug the appliances, shut off the water to the washer and check the automatic light switch to see if it is set to turn on the lights later.

He wouldn't appreciate her honking at him while he was running around like a chicken with his head cut off, trying to leave the house for the outing and checking everything before they go. Horn honkers are for the road, not the driveway. The thoughtful thing for him to do would be to get out of the car and go in the house to help her. It's not going to kill him. She's probably ready to kill him though, and if he continues to honk at her, it will ruin her day, and their outing. It's just not worth honking and ruining the day. Don't you agree?

29 JEALOUSY— THE GREEN-EYED MONSTER

He gets nervous whenever she is not with him. He is so possessive that he is dying inside. He thinks she just does not understand. Oh, but yes, she does understand. He is totally out of control—he needs to know where she is every minute, making her accountable for every move she makes when he is not with her. He does not sound like the type of man that she is looking to spend the rest of her life. He is psychologically dangerous for her. He is trying to control her.

She cannot go to parties with him and talk to other men because he is so threatened. This is the "green-eyed monster," jealousy. She feels like she is in prison. She is always with him and he still does not trust her. If a relationship is real solid, no one can come between them. Being jealous is not the answer to a good relationship, it is the trust that makes it work, and trust takes time. If she is a flirt and it makes him uncomfortable, then he needs to tell her and if she continues, he needs a new girlfriend. Simple as that. Life is too short to be miserable, and some people just do not bring out the best in each other. Jealousy will have an opposite effect on her. It will make her think he is not a secure man, and therefore less desirable in her eyes. Jealousy is immature. She wants someone who is in control of his emotions and jealousy is an out of control emotion.

30 THE POINTER

When he gets excited during a discussion, out comes that index finger and he puts it right in her face. This is rude and unnecessary, and not a good way for him to express himself if he is upset or trying to "make a point." Better watch out, she might bite it and then he'd really be sore. He can make his point without pointing.

31 WASH OUT HIS MOUTH

He has made a really good first impression on her. He looks great, smells great, is dressed handsomely, and he seems like a real gentleman. Then he opens his mouth and ruins everything.

When he gets angry and mad, his mouth gets dirty and bad. Laughingly, he told her how, as a child, he got his mouth washed out with soap when he used a word out of his little collection of "those words," the (hell, shit, damn) words. Well, he's all grown now and he's added yet another wonderful word, "the 'f' word" to his vocabulary. This is a total turnoff and shows that he has no class.

He is a dad now. He has a little boy, Johnny, and Johnny just got suspended from school because he repeated one of those words that Dad uses. Dad thinks Johnny should do as he says, and not do as he does. But Johnny sees it as Monkey See, Monkey Do. Children are mimics, and Dad might consider setting a better example. He needs to wash his own mouth out with soap, not Johnny's.

32 YELLER, SCREAMER, THUMPER

He might have been the loud, mouthy bully of the neighborhood. Maybe he was the quiet one that never said much, but if he got upset, he would take a swing at you, and you were decked. Remember him? Everybody has known one of these guys in their lifetime. "The Pressure Cooker," we have learned to call him. You just never know what is going to set him off. Pretty scary, actually. And these days, you never know—he could even be carrying a weapon. A frightening man to be involved with. He can make a woman physically and emotionally sick, because she never knows when he will explode and what little thing might set him off. The man who does not keep his cool will destroy any relationship he has with a woman. His explosions of anger when he gets out of control chip away at the very cement that bonds the relationship. Perhaps as a child he saw his father yell, scream, or thump on his mother. Now he thinks it is okay for him to do the same thing. This is not acceptable anytime or anywhere. We all get angry, but we need to learn how to vent anger without abusing our loved ones. He should go take a walk, count to ten, or leave the room. A real man does not get out of control and yell, scream, and thump the woman he loves. Sometimes it is hard not to raise a voice, but hitting a woman does not accomplish anything.

If he is upset and hit her, he could permanently hurt her. A man who would hit a woman may also hit a child. And spanking a child is a very delicate thing. Slapping his hands or on the back of his leg and telling him 'no' is adequate. Do not ever slap a child in the face or on his tailbone. This could injure the child for life. Here again, he should take time out and go for a walk or leave the room until he calms down. Things take on a different perspective after the initial "heated moment" cools down. If he loves someone, that person should be the last one he wants to hurt. Cool guys keep their cool...

33 THE KNUCKLE AND JOINT CRACKER

Snap, crackle, pop! This isn't his cereal we're speaking of here. He's rotating his poor neck and popping it, round and around he goes. He's going to get whiplash if he's not careful. Crunch, crunch, now it's his fingers. Between cracking his neck and then his knuckles, the sound is making her crazy. It would be like her running her fingernails down the blackboard. It makes the hair on the back of her neck stand up. It gives her the creeps. Plus, it makes the knuckles at the joints bow out and they get larger. It's really hard to get a ring over those huge knuckles. They not only get bigger, but as he gets older, quite possibly he may develop a joint disorder. Then he'd really be cracked.

34 HE NEVER GETS SICK

That's what he says, he never gets sick. Therefore, he does not need to go to the doctor. Right? Wrong. He takes his automobile in for a tune-up (examination), so why doesn't he treat his body (which he cannot trade in, in five years) as well as he treats his automobile? This is not smart, this is bad judgment. A regular physical examination might save his life. He used to think that going to the doctor was "not macho." Well, I'll tell you what. Macho never was very smart. Smart is to go and get those regular parts checked out, because most of his parts can't be replaced easily as an automobile's. An ounce of prevention is worth a pound of cure. He needs to be a real "smart" man and get himself to see the "Doc" at least once a year. Say Ahh!

35 THE CHIMNEY

He'll huff and he'll puff until he blows the house (I mean her) down. He hasn't heeded the Surgeon General's warning that tells him, "Yes, cigarettes, cigars, and chewing tobacco do cause cancer." And the passive smoke is injurious too. Now, if it's so bad, then why is he exposing his wife, children or grandchildren to an unhealthy bad habit? Slowly killing himself by smoking is one thing, but exposing others is selfish. So, go huff and puff and blow out that cigarette.

36 THE FINGER THUMPER AND PENCIL RAPPER

He's decided to go out for lunch. He sat down at his table and is so anxious to get back to the office that he's becoming quite impatient waiting for his food to come. He begins thumping his fingers on the table, thump 2-3-4, thump 2-3-4. He's just so uptight.

He needs to take a break and sit back, *relax*, take a deep breath and put his brain in a beautiful, tranquil setting somewhere with the woman of his dreams. Yeah, that's right. *Relax*. I'm sure he's got to be aware that *stress* is the No. 1 killer of men. He has to take care of that heart of his or else he'll have a...you guessed it, the biggy...Heart Attack!

Lunch is over and he's made it back to his office. He's sitting behind his desk, with his pencil now in his hand, rap, rap, rapping away. The more pressure he puts on himself, (and he's the only one who can turn it off), the more intense he becomes, the faster and harder he raps his poor pencil. The deeper in thought he goes, his pencil somehow makes it to his mouth. He begins chewing and sucking on the eraser. Pencil lead is poisonous and for health reasons he certainly doesn't want to poison himself. A man wants to keep "pencil in hand" not in his mouth.

37 HE'S FORGOTTEN HIS PLEASE AND THANK YOU'S

Politeness seems to be something of the past. It seems as though someone just dug a big hole, buried and forgot them. Whatever happened to "please," "would you please," "please pass the food," "thank you for the nice dinner," "thank you for the nice day," "thank you for being there," or just plain "Thank you?" Life has become so fast-paced, he tends to abbreviate words, and now has even left out his 'please' and 'thank you's'. It makes her feel special to hear those important little words. She will naturally want to do more for him when he uses them. He needs to brush up on his 'please' and 'thank you's' and put them back into his vocabulary. And if she doesn't use them, a friendly reminder is in order. What's good for the goose is good for the gander!

38 LUMBER IN HIS MOUTH

The restaurants always have them at the register for him, all wrapped in plastic. They usually have no taste, are cream-colored, and about three inches long. No, it is not a saltine cracker. It's a toothpick! He grabs one on the way out the door and she has to watch him pick his leftover food out of his teeth all night long (not real sexy), or suck on it and try to talk with it in his mouth at the same time.

A better way for him to deal with food in his teeth would be to go to the men's restroom before he leaves the restaurant and take care of the problem right then, so it does not bother him the rest of the evening. Now, when she goes to the ladies room, he can go to the men's room and use some dental floss. There are small, compact dental floss containers he can purchase and carry in his pocket, or he can put a piece from home in his wallet (with his other personals). That way, he will never have to be embarrassed with food in his teeth again. Have floss, will travel! Smile.

39 THE DISRESPECTFUL AND FAST DRIVER

He fantasizes about racing in the Indy 500, and he tries to fulfill these fantasies on the road, with her in the passenger seat. Not fun for her at all when he is in control and she's not. She's frightened and will not say anything because she does not want to seem uncool. He's trying to impress her, and she is really not impressed. Whoever equated fast driving in a regular automobile as being cool has obviously never witnessed a death or a crippling accident resulting from an automobile accident. She wants him to show her how responsible he is, not what a jerk he is by driving fast and recklessly. Some men use cars as props. They are their alter-egos. It is cool on a track, if it is his profession to drive fast, but it's not cool to end up a cripple or dead due to a car accident by driving too fast and reckless.

He also might be courteous to others on the road and not yell and scream so others don't shoot at him. It is safer today to be nice. Try it, you might like it—and live longer too!

40 HIS OIL-LEAKING CAR

She's so excited and proud of her new home. Her new place even has its own driveway with an attached garage entrance. She'd thrilled to know she won't have a long walk from her car to her front door anymore. She can just open the garage door with her new garage door opener and pull right in. Great!

The carpet is clean and new, spotless, the paint on the walls smells fresh and the driveway was, too...Until he parked his leaky car in her driveway and left her with an oil mess to have to clean up. This isn't a lady's favorite thing, greasy oil, you know.

He might always consider parking on the street in front of her home instead of in her new driveway since his car may leak oil. If she doesn't care about the oil on her driveway, she'll tell him to go ahead and park in her driveway. If she does care, at least he was polite enough to park on the street and let the oil drop on the asphalt and not on her nice new driveway. If his car leaks at home, I'm sure it's not going to stop at her house just because he's there. He could plug it up with a cork or put a big diaper on it. Just kidding...

41 THE KNEE WIGGLER

Up and down, up and down, up and down...He's sitting across from her and she is trying to concentrate on what he is saying, but she cannot. She is completely preoccupied with watching his crossed leg move up and down, and up and down. The proper way for a man to sit is not with his knees crossed. The proper way is to lay the ankle of one leg on the knee of the opposite leg. This way he cannot wiggle. Anyway, men are not suppose to wiggle, women are!

42 THE MAN THAT WON'T HELP

The idea that a man does not help around the house at all is primitive, especially now since husband and wife usually both work outside the home, and maybe now, too, they also have children...Speaking of children, it is amazing how he offers to watch them for her when she needs to go do something like shopping, getting a haircut, etc. All of a sudden they are her kids. Uh, Uh, Uh....

Now, if the woman chooses to stay home, then her job is to take care of the home. If she is lucky enough that she can have a cleaning lady or service come in and clean, well, good for her. And even if she does, there are still many other duties the woman has to tend to, such as laundry, marketing, cooking, banking, paying bills, running errands, decorating or re-decorating, social entertaining and engagements, and, of course, if there are children, that is a whole other job, all in itself.

Hopefully, he learned how to share when he was about 2 years old. Sharing responsibilities takes the burden off each other. However he chooses to delegate the chores, he might try and think of her and whether or not her load is too heavy. Sometimes if her load is too heavy, the relationship becomes lopsided, and she gets cranky. So let's just say he needs to practice teamwork—he is the center, and she is the quarterback. She can't play the game until the ball is hiked to her. The game needs more than one person to play it. She's not the game, she's only a key player. There are no prima donnas in a well-played football game. A quarterback is only as good as the center that hikes her the ball so she can execute her pass. Relationships that work are like a good football game—it's called teamwork. Yeah!

43 CHANNEL CHANGER

Flip, flip, flip, flip, it flips 56 times. No, it's not the pages of his latest book he is flipping through, it is the famous remote control box for his television that he has in his hand, and he is continuously changing the channels. After two or three rounds of the channels changing, she gets disinterested in watching, and will probably make a comment. He asked her to sit down and watch a program with him, not to try and watch 56 at one time. So, let's make a decision men, either the American League or the National League! Which is it?

44 MR. SILENCE—THE POUTER

She might as well be a statue or the wall, because that's just the way he treats her when he is upset—like she is an inanimate object, nonexistent. So, he's upset...Maybe it was her, maybe not. Maybe it was an employee, a co-worker, or someone who cut him off on the freeway. Whatever it was, he is not talking, period. He does not even make eye contact. He is withdrawn. This is absolutely no fun for her.

Instead of addressing the problem, this is how he chooses to cope. Silence is not golden in this case. It is better for him to air his grievances than to hold them in. It always feels better to talk about it, even if he thinks it is a trivial problem. Nothing is that bad that he should totally ignore her. Besides, there is nothing he can do about the problem that has already happened, because it is just that—already done. He might try and improve his negative thoughts to positive ones, so that he can decide how to solve the problem. Life is full of all kinds of ups and downs; it is a roller coaster ride. Nobody said it was going to be easy...

Circumstances happen, and sometimes when one door closes, another one opens. When that door does open, it is better to be there with a smile, rather than a scowl. As he goes through life and realizes that life is not to be taken too seriously, but rather looked upon as an experience, he is a much happier and well-adjusted man. A good sense of humor is a real treasure. So, let's go for the gold and learn to laugh at ourselves...and be happy...Life is so precious, and a day of being angry, is a day wasted!

45 HIDING BEHIND THE PAPER

She thought she saw him come to the table for breakfast, but now he's disappeared. As soon as he sat down, he immediately dove into his newspaper and hasn't come up for air, let alone any sort of conversation. She thought she said breakfast for two, not one. Unfortunately, he's so indulged in his newspaper, that he hasn't even noticed the oatmeal, juice and toast she just put in front of him. How depressing.

She sits down to share their breakfast, and she might as well be all alone. He reads, she sighs. She talks, he grunts.

The oatmeal is getting colder and thicker by the minute. Messy, gooey situation.

Reading the newspaper is admirable and very educational. But the table is not the best place when someone else is present. Before or after the meal in the living room, den, or maybe even in the privacy of his bathroom would be better.

A wall of paper between two intimates is not very cozy after awhile. He knows what I mean.

Oh, and men...Don't forget the newsprint gets all over the hands. A little soap and water after reading the paper is a good idea. It keeps the light switches cleaner. Also, the newsprint does rub off on the cushions of the white couch, so be sure to keep the paper on the floor. Thanks for being considerate.

46 WALL MAULER

This man seems to have a problem keeping his hands to himself. You'll find him leaning on the walls with his hands, rounding the corners of the freshly painted walls with his hands and swinging in the doorway jams. You might see a monkey at the zoo doing these things, but this is not favorable Monkey See, Monkey Do. This is undesirable Monkey Business. So stop it!

47 MR. MESSY— THE CLOTHES DROPPER

This man hasn't discovered the dirty-clothes hamper or hangers—yet. As soon as he hits the door, off come the shoes, then the shirt and then his pants. Undressing himself and just dropping them as he goes. Now, who do you suppose is going to pick up these articles before someone trips over them or they gather dust? Not her.

The smartest way to remedy this problem would be for him to at least make it to the closet and take off the shoes, (so now a least they are in the closet), then finish undressing, and put the dirty clothes in the hamper or in a plastic bag if he doesn't have a hamper in the closet. It is not a good idea to put anything wet or damp in the hamper or bag, because if it's left there, it will generate mold on his clothes. Wet bath towels shouldn't be put in a hamper or left on a mattress. It will leave water rings on his new mattress and it will rot from too much moisture. He needs to hang up those towels to dry right after he showers. This way, his dirty clothes won't mildew and leave his closet or hamper smelling foul. If the hamper gets that way, he should spray it with a disinfectant and air it out for a day or two. The mildew is unhealthy to breathe and will make you sick. So, clean it up guys!

48 THE A-BOMB APARTMENT

She went over to visit him and when he opened the door, it looked like a tornado had hit his apartment. Dirty dishes in the kitchen and dining room, newspapers all over the place, dust an inch thick on the furniture, the carpet filthy, and the baseboards not white anymore because they hadn't ever been vacuumed. The kitchen floor was so sticky that her tennis shoes stuck to it. She had to use the bathroom and she almost vomited when she had to use the toilet. It had a black ring in the bowl and the seat was up, exposing urine stains all over the rim and all over the floor. It reeked of urine because he is a bad shot. If he would just sit on the toilet at home and urinate, then he wouldn't have this problem. Urinals in a public restroom are different, and he can stand up. But at home, because a woman has to use (and generally clean) the toilet also, it would be nice for h[illegible] not to have to clean up after him like she would for a child. If he misses, the tissue is right there next to him. How about wiping it off? I mean if it was the other way around guys, would you like to have to deal with this problem? I really doubt it.

Take an hour or so a week and clean up that place. It's not enjoyable, and makes her uncomfortable to be entertained in an environment like this. Everybody likes a clean and tidy place; it's just that some men are just lazy or will give the excuse, "I don't have the time." She works full-time and her apartment is clean because she "makes" time. She'll respect him more if he takes care of himself and his home. No woman wants a man she has to clean up after. She has enough to do taking care of her place and her own things. If he takes care of his things and she takes care of hers, they have a lot more quality time together, happy, and not fighting. Touche. No boxing gloves tonight!

49 HE LEFT THE SEAT UP, SHE FELL IN

He got into this habit when he was young, and when he moved in by himself, it carried over. Now, he's living with a woman and last week in the middle of the night, she got up to go to the bathroom, went to sit down on the toilet, and fell in because the seat was up, and got stuck. The Fire Department was called at four o'clock in the morning to get her out. They broke the commode to get her out. Pretty embarrassing for her. So men, let's really try and remember, there are other people who use the toilet, too. Try and be more considerate and put the seat down. She'll thank you very much.

50 THE WORKAHOLIC

Nine to Five, Nine to Five...Remember those words, because he has forgotten them.

A man works a lot for one of three reasons: One, he has just started a new business and he is trying to get it off and running, so he's putting in a lot of extra hours. The second reason could be that he has a boss~who wants him to work overtime constantly, to get certain things done that he, the boss, does not want to do himself. (And these bosses are usually real egomaniacs. Always delegating all his work to other people and not paying them overtime.) And the third reason he doesn't come home and works so much, is because he really does not want to be at home. This could be because of a lot of other reasons. Maybe his wife is a nag and he does not want to deal with her. Or the children are small and cry a lot and he cannot deal with that. Or, maybe he has in-law problems, or the "biggy"—money problems. Whatever it is that he isn't dealing with, he needs to open his mouth and try to calmly discuss it. If these problems manifest themselves, they will permanently damage and undermine what was once a beautiful love affair. Sometimes the solutions to these problems are not always immediate, but by discussing them, he can release the steam of the pressure-cooker—him!

51 THE ALCOHOLIC

He tells her he doesn't have a problem with alcohol, yet he drinks and wakes up with these tremendous headaches. "It's not a hangover," he insists; he must have eaten something last night that did not agree with him. Right! Oh, and did he really say those things? No, he didn't, he says, vehemently defending himself. And then he pops her one. No, not him. "Oh, I guess I had a little too much last night." A little too much. How about just too much, period? Poor Me, Poor Me, would you pour me another drink? Does he come around in the morning, instead of wake up in the morning? Does he fall asleep at night, or pass out?

A true test to see if he has a problem: If he can drink only 2 drinks a day for 30 days, he has control of his drinking. If not, he has a problem. Alcoholics Anonymous is a wonderful place to begin a new life of sobriety. She might suggest he go to a meeting, before he has an accident and kills someone. It happens all the time. A drunk driver killing someone else's mother, sister, father, brother, daughter or son. And, if he is drinking at home and has a problem, he is not setting a good example for his children.

He has seen it in the paper and heard it on the radio many times. A boy of 18 is killed on graduation night. Doesn't Dad always celebrate everything with alcohol? The young man is graduating, and drinking is real manly and grown-up. Dad does it, and he's cool and successful, so therefore drinking must be cool...His child finished high school, and alcohol finished his child's life.

He drinks to be someone else. Obviously he has pain and anger to need the escape. He needs to get real with himself. Alcohol is a dangerous and addictive escape. There are other alternatives. Exercise and stress management are better alternatives.

A successful man is like a race horse. He would not give his race horse alcohol before a big race, so why would he drink and lose his edge in business? Something to think about, wouldn't you say?

52 THE FOODAHOLIC

He eats and eats and always talks about how he wants to shed those extra twenty pounds and start exercising. He talks a good game, but she need not hold her breath, because it usually is just that—talk.

Everything he does in his life, he celebrates with food. He rewards himself with food: the big deal, the hole-in-one, it's Friday night~, company over, the nine o'clock movie, Christmas, Thanksgiving, his vacation or his birthday.

He still eats everything on his plate, just like his mother told him to do as a child. He has learned some bad habits that he needs to improve. He needs to practice some behavior modification and find out the reasons why he overeats in order to control his overeating. Staying in shape and being healthy is a daily practice that has to be acknowledged. Overeating is as much an addiction as alcohol or drugs. He needs to learn to read labels and be aware of the fat and sodium content. He might compare other products so that he will know which one is the best.

He might eat until he is satisfied, not stuffed. He doesn't have to finish everything on his plate, either. And if he wants a "goody," he might eat less at a meal and then he can add that special treat once a week. Americans tend to have no self-discipline, especially where food is concerned. He spoils himself "too much" and hasn't learned the words "No, I can't have it." He needs to remember whatever he eats excessively, he is going to wear later.

53 THE DRUGAHOLIC

For her to try and have a good, solid relationship with him would be about as safe as her holding a lit stick of dynamite and having someone telling her it will not explode. Yeah, right. And, the sky is green and the grass is blue. And he probably has told her everything in moderation. Not where drugs are concerned. It may start out innocently, but it does not stay that way. It is always a little bit more and more and more. Before long it is a full-blown, expensive habit. He does not realize that every time he smokes, snorts or shoots up, it is money down the toilet and that he is ruining his body. It is a chicken's way of escape. He thinks he is so cool, but he's really screwed up. He might take the money he is spending on drugs and use it for medical help. This way he'll keep his mind and body. Using drugs is a slow death—like cancer, it eats away at all those vital organs. It is hard to function when half of your brain is gone. Recreational drugs are for losers and weak men.

54 JOCKOHOLIC

He talks about the good ol' days, still lives in the "college jock syndrome," and won't let go. She listens as he tells his stories over and over again, about how great he was in sports in high school and college (she really doesn't care). He lives in the past and tries to keep up and do the same things he did when he was eighteen. His back is out of whack, his knees hurt all the time, and he still tries to get out there with the boys. He might want to consider trying a new sport, one that is a little easier on his back and knees, and realize that time marches on, and he can't do everything he did when he was younger with so much intensity. He might consider swimming, biking, or golfing as an alternative, and then she can play too! Fore...

55 GYMAHOLIC

He is so narcissistic about his body that there isn't a mirror in the world that hasn't seen him admire himself. Going to the gym three days a week for an hour is enough for a man to stay in shape. A healthy "tight" and "toned" body is sexy, and some definition is highly desirable, but most women find a body that is too big and pumped up looks freaky and weird. Some men equate huge muscles with sexuality, and the bigger the muscles are, the more of a man they are. Wrong. Their confidence comes from seeing themselves get bigger by the day. Perhaps this man has a sexual dysfunction, low self-esteem, or just maybe a small unit. It is not what he has in his pants, it is how special he makes her feel that is most important to her. Don't forget it!

Too much of anything is not good. Going to the gym all the time can be as much of an addiction as drugs. All things in moderation. See you at the gym.

WOW!
JACK WHITE

56 THE SEXAHOLIC

He never gets enough. Three to four times a day. He is an addict, and yes, has a real problem. This addiction is just as bad as alcohol or drugs, because he is always looking for the next victim to conquer. And, chances are, he's also kinky. It's not love he's looking for, it's sex. In this day and age he can be a pretty dangerous fellow, with AIDS and all. He's always on the make and it's a thought that he is preoccupied with, constantly. Not a well-rounded man, this one. A real heartbreaker he can be, because women mistake his prowess as "he really loves me" and, "yes, I'm the one he wants. I'm the one who can fulfill him and keep him." No one woman can keep this man's interest for too long because he has a real dysfunctional problem. She can never help him, because he needs some real heavy duty sex counseling. A woman who tries, will only fail. She will end up being another victim, a win for him a loss for her. She best pass up "Mr. Ronnie Romance," unless all she is after is a fleeting moment of empty, non-meaningful, calculated movements and words.

57 THE OGLER

Back and forth, up and down...No, it's not his television's vertical and horizontal adjustment we are talking about here, it's his darting eyes and out-of-control rotating head that are trying to get a peek at every woman that passes by him. This is fine, as long as he isn't in the company of another woman, even if she is only a friend. This is rude and totally disrespectful, so "cool it!"

58 MR. TOO PERFECT

He's such a perfectionist that nobody can live with his obsessive-compulsive behavior. There is neat and tidy, and then there's the crazy-maker. It's almost impossible to live peacefully with someone like him, unless she is just like him. A disorganized, lazy woman would never make it with this man. Even a normal woman would have a hard time.

Men who are like this outwardly are not in control of their lives and feel disorganized inside. He tries to keep control on the inside by trying to keep everything in place, organized and clean on the outside. I know a woman whose husband would wad up his shirts after she ironed them and throw them on the floor because they weren't ironed well enough. Can you imagine? And if he didn't like the meal she cooked, he'd dump it over on the table on the place mat. Not nice. This marriage is now over.

These men don't know how to have a good time and enjoy life. Their life is too organized. They cannot be spontaneous. Before they go somewhere, everything needs to be done before they can have fun. A real type "A" personality, and a real crazy-maker. He'll live longer and be much more fun to be around if he relaxes a little more. Heart attacks are real common among these types. He needs to try not being so much in control. It takes less energy, and he'll enjoy life much more.

59 THE MAN WITH CLASS—THE ATTENTIVE ONE

Class is not something he wears, something he drives, where he lives or went to school, or how much money he is worth. Class is his presence, his whole state of being. Just his presence alone commands respect. He's not flashy or loud, he's rather reserved, has a great sense of humor, and a real good sense of well-being about himself.

When he is with a real lady (not just a woman, I said a lady), he attends to her because he's treating her like a lady and real ladies love it. He will open her car door, her doors, pull her chair out at the table to seat or excuse her, stand when she leaves the room, and he will walk to the outside of her on the street to protect her in a most gallant manner.

Many young and ambitious women (especially young, idealistic college grads) feel that this sort of treatment is chauvinistic. Well, that's their problem. Being polite and attentive to a lady is not saying she is less than his equal, rather it is showing respect and being very gallant. And if she has a problem with this, talk to her when she's 40 and wants to get married and can't figure out why men aren't attracted to her. It's because the thing he loves the most about a woman, her femininity, has never been developed.

She's too busy trying to act like a man. She can look like a woman and dress like a woman, but if she doesn't act feminine, then he will have a hard time relating to her in a romantic situation. He might as well be with one of the guys. A woman can be successful without acting like a man. It's called being assertive, not aggressive, firm but not coarse, harsh or loud. And being a 'yes' person, does not make her feminine. She can still be feminine and say she doesn't agree with him. She wants respect and to be able to voice her opinions. She has a right to her own opinions. He needs to listen and respect her opinions even if he doesn't agree. If he doesn't listen, she will become frustrated and turn her frustrations inward and then they won't ever have open lines of communication, and this is the beginning of the end of their relationship.

Unless she's a lesbian or a "ball-buster," an attentive man is every woman's dream. An unexpected card means more than anything to a woman who is sentimental—and most every woman is sentimental! A small gift, it doesn't have to be anything big and expensive, like a dozen red roses. How about one rose? Or stop at the candy store and buy her one piece of chocolate. It doesn't have to be a big box of candy. It's really the thought that counts, especially if she watches her weight.

Just to know that he took the time out of his busy day to remember her, will tickle her more than anything. A card, a flower, a piece of candy—that's really all she wants. So little can mean so much. Try it, you'll see what I mean.

60 THE BALANCED MAN

He is every woman's Prince Charming. He is a man who keeps life in its proper perspective, no matter what happens. Self-assured, he commands respect. This man's middle name is integrity. He would rather have people respect him than like him. His morals and principles are irreproachable, and that goes without saying. He's very definitive about his direction and goals in his life. He is a proud man with real values.

He learned a long time ago that a sense of humor reigns supreme. He's learned not to take life too seriously and can laugh at himself as well. He's not loud and boisterous; no "razzle-dazzle" with this man. He has no need to impress others. He knows to keep his personal wealth to himself, because he learned the value of privacy earlier in his life and understands that jealousy is universal among peers. He would never boast about himself; his self-confidence just oozes from under his skin.

Character, well this man has lots of it. He has a special quality about him that she's attracted to, and she can sense he is very different. He is an experience. And yes, he has faults, but his character is so wonderful, his few faults are endurable.

There is a pleasantness in his nature. He thinks before he reacts in a negative, angry way. He's in control of his actions, in all situations. He would never make a fool out of himself by over-reacting and embarrassing himself and others close to him. He is rational under all circumstances.

He is a good listener and knows the smartest men in the world have learned the importance of listening. He doesn't talk just to hear himself talk. He listens in earnest to what she has to say, and becomes interested, even if he doesn't agree. He respects her thoughts and opinions, even if they are different than his. Most men cannot do that. A real man appreciates a woman with a mind, and one who has her own opinions. He doesn't ever try to control her. He encourages her to develop her life. He lets her be what she wants to be because he is secure within himself. He is not ever jealous of her and he has learned the word "trust."

This man says what he means, and means what he says. His word is as solid as a rock. He values all people, and doesn't look down on those less fortunate than him. He knows there is a place with pride for every person, no matter what he does for a living. Every person this man knows, has value to him or her. He makes everyone feel special.

He is an honest man in both his personal and business life, and has learned to never burn bridges along the way, because he never knows when he may have dealings with that person at another time.

He's a home entertainment center all by himself, but enjoys being with her. He gives her time to do her "girl" things. He never holds on to her too tightly, because he knows this is not healthy for their relationship. He appreciates quality rather than quantity with women. She is an anchor for him in their relationship, and he lets her know how important a part she plays in his life. They are a couple, and couples do most things together. The family that plays together, stays together.

He is highly competitive at work, but he leaves his competitive spirit there. He can play a game of tennis or golf with her, and if she wins, he doesn't get upset. He understands that the reason they are playing together is to be just that, together.

To be admired and respected, he realizes that he should always set a good example. He never gets out of control with alcohol, nor does he drugs. A woman feels safe with him, and she knows he will protect her. He is considerate of her and understands when she is sick. And if she has "PMS," he realizes that sometimes she may get cranky because of that horrible time of the month she dislikes so immensely.

He shares his confidences and experiences with her, and is comfortable enough with her to know she won't use them against him if they have a quarrel. If they do quarrel, he fights fairly and doesn't bring up "old dirt." He sticks to the subject at hand.

There is no perfect man, only one who strives for it. He always makes an effort, no matter how impossible he thinks it will be. This man doesn't chase rainbows, but takes the challenge, goes for the gold, and usually finds them both: his rainbow and his gold.

A smart man will let a good woman be his conscience! Think about it...

The End